VICTORIOUS *Living*

Allyson Rola

Cover Design and Content Layout By: Catalyst Media
creatingcatalyst.com

Library of Congress Cataloging-in-Publication Data

ISBN: 978-1535008112
Printed in the United States of America

So shall my word be that goes forth from my mouth; It shall not return to me void, But it shall accomplish what I please, And it shall prosper in the thing for which I sent it.
—*Isaiah 55:11*

I pray that as you read through this book you will begin to realize that whatever you are in need of, Jesus has already supplied it for you on the cross.

With love,
Ally

CONTENTS

INTRODUCTION

I was home for the weekend, driving from place to place, when the Lord laid the idea for this book on my heart. It's funny. He will speak to you wherever you are—whatever you are doing. You just have to be listening. He will even give you an idea to write a book while you're stopped at a red light!

At the age of nine, I lost all of my hair to an incurable disease, Alopecia Universalis. Years later (13 to be exact), I got a revelation of God's healing power. I began to meditate on His Word. It is so powerful! His Word brings health!

Scriptures began to jump out at me! Psalms 103:1-3 literally changed my life. "He heals all of my diseases," it proclaims. I believed those verses and received full restoration. I am so grateful for divine health. I am so grateful for the full head of hair I now have. It is proof to me that the Lord really did accomplish what He said He accomplished. It is proof He is alive and active.

I would read healing scriptures over and over again. I renewed my mind to the fact that He healed all of my diseases.

This book is special. It was written for you. God had YOU in mind when He dropped the idea for this book on my heart. If you need healing, turn to the pages on healing, and read the verses over and over. If you need to get out of debt, turn to the pages on prosperity, and read those verses over and over. Whatever you need, find a verse to stand on, and make it your own!

The Lord is at work in your life. He is moving. Today, begin to renew your mind to all the Lord has for you.

DIRECTION

Sometimes life can get complicated. It seems like there are a million different choices we could make all in one day. Even the decision of the color to paint your room can become tedious when you realize how many different paint colors there are. Well, I have good news for you. The Lord has a plan for your life. He cares about the details. He cares about the outfit you will put on tomorrow. He cares about the job you have. He even cares about the paint color for your room. Ask the Lord, He will answer you.

> *Trust in the LORD with all thine heart; and lean not unto thine own understanding. In all thy ways acknowledge him, and he shall direct thy paths.*
> *—Proverbs 3:5-6*

> *The secret of the Lord is with them that fear him; and he will shew them his covenant.*
> *—Psalms 25:14*

> *But as it is written, Eye hath not seen, nor ear heard, neither have entered into the heart of man, the things which God hath*

prepared for them that love him. But God hath revealed them unto us by his Spirit: for the Spirit searcheth all things, yea, the deep things of God.

—1 Corinthians 2:9-10

For as many as are led by the Spirit of God, they are the sons of God.

—Romans 8:14

I will instruct thee and teach thee in the way which thou shalt go: I will guide thee with mine eye.

—Psalms 32:8

For I know the thoughts that I think toward you, saith the Lord, thoughts of peace, and not of evil, to give you an expected end.

—Jeremiah 29:11

He restoreth my soul: he leadeth me in the paths of righteousness for his name's sake.

—Psalms 23:3

Thus saith the Lord, which maketh a way in the sea, and a path in the mighty waters; Which bringeth forth the chariot and horse, the army and the power; they shall lie down together, they shall not rise: they are extinct, they are quenched as tow. Remember ye not the former things, neither consider the things of old. Behold, I will do a new thing; now it shall spring forth; shall ye not know it? I will even make a way in the wilderness, and rivers in the desert.

—Isaiah 43:16-19

Even if you are in the desert place, the Lord will lead you and supply all of your needs. He will direct your every step. He has a plan for your life, and if you listen, you will hear His voice.

My sheep hear my voice, and I know them, and they follow me.

—John 10:27

Also I heard the voice of the Lord, saying, Whom shall I send, and who will go for us? Then said I, Here am I; send me.

—Isaiah 6:8

What? know ye not that your body is the temple of the Holy Ghost which is in you, which ye have of God, and ye are not your own?

—1 Corinthians 6:19

The God of the entire universe dwells inside of YOU. Wherever you go, He goes! What an honor! He is constantly speaking to you and leading you.

And thine ears shall hear a word behind thee, saying, This is the way, walk ye in it, when ye turn to the right hand, and when ye turn to the left.

—Isaiah 30:21

Notes

Notes

Notes

FAVOR

Every morning I say out loud, "Favor surrounds me like a shield." Sometimes I just sit and think, *what does it look like for the God of the universe to favor me!?* Some days it looks like having an extra long lunch break, other days it looks like getting a check in the mail. Soon it will look like a handsome man of godly character.

Literally, the creator of the entire universe favors YOU. You are surrounded by His favor. Don't get so busy that you don't see it at work in your life.

When your boss walks in at the exact moment you are doing an awesome job– favor. When you are given a surprise gift in the mail–favor. When you get the closest parking spot at the grocery store–favor. Open your eyes to His favor today. The more you see it, the more of it you'll receive!

For the Lord God is a sun and shield; the Lord bestows favor and honor; no good thing does he withhold from those whose walk is blameless

—Psalms 84:11 (NIV)

As Christians, when God looks at us, He sees Jesus. Our past, present, and future sins have all been forgiven. When Christ said it is finished on the cross 2,000 years ago, He provided for us everything we will ever need. We can now come to the throne of God blameless. We are righteous through Christ:

> *For he hath made him to be sin for us, who knew no sin; that we might be made the righteousness of God in him.*
> *—1 Corinthians 5:21*

> *For as by one man's disobedience many were made sinners, so by the obedience of one shall many be made righteous.*
> *—Romans 5:19*

Because of what Christ did for us on the cross, we are considered righteous! We are living under the new covenant! In Deuteronomy 28, it talks about the blessings that will come upon you if you obey. Those promises are for us!

> *And all these blessings shall come on thee, and overtake thee, if thou shalt hearken unto the voice of the Lord thy God. Blessed shalt thou be in the city, and blessed shalt thou be in the field. Blessed shall be the fruit of thy body, and the fruit of thy ground, and the fruit of thy cattle, the increase of thy kine, and the flocks of thy sheep. Blessed shall be thy basket and thy store. Blessed shalt thou be when thou*

comest in, and blessed shalt thou be when thou goest out. The Lord shall cause thine enemies that rise up against thee to be smitten before thy face: they shall come out against thee one way, and flee before thee seven ways. The Lord shall command the blessing upon thee in thy storehouses, and in all that thou settest thine hand unto; and he shall bless thee in the land which the Lord thy God giveth thee. The Lord shall establish thee an holy people unto himself, as he hath sworn unto thee, if thou shalt keep the commandments of the Lord thy God, and walk in his ways. And all people of the earth shall see that thou art called by the name of the Lord; and they shall be afraid of thee. And the Lord shall make thee plenteous in goods, in the fruit of thy body, and in the fruit of thy cattle, and in the fruit of thy ground, in the land which the Lord sware unto thy fathers to give thee. The Lord shall open unto thee his good treasure, the heaven to give the rain unto thy land in his season, and to bless all the work of thine hand: and thou shalt lend unto many nations, and thou shalt not borrow. And the Lord shall make thee the head, and not the tail; and thou shalt be above only, and thou shalt not be beneath; if that thou hearken unto the commandments of the Lord thy God, which I command thee this day, to observe and to do them:
—Deuteronomy 28:2-13

Knowing our identity in Christ is so important! We are righteous, forgiven, healed, prosperous, loved, and favored! Everything we will ever need has already been provided for!

> **For thou, Lord, wilt bless the righteous; with favour wilt thou compass him as with a shield.**
> **—Psalms 5:12**

His favor surrounds us like a shield! When you are looking for a job, know His favor is surrounding you!

I was working as an admissions counselor in Connecticut when the Lord called me to go to Charis Bible College Charlotte. I had to leave my job and trust that the Lord had another job for me in South Carolina. It wasn't even a month into my move when I was offered a job that worked perfectly with my schedule!

When you know your identity, you will begin to see His favor work in every area of your life, including your job!

> *For his anger lasts only a moment, but his favor lasts a lifetime; weeping may stay for the night, but rejoicing comes in the morning.*
> *—Psalms 30:5 (NIV)*

At work one day, my co-worker was talking about how the president's daughter got a very competitive internship. Most of the people listening rolled their eyes and stated things like,

"Of course she did; she's the president's daughter!" After hearing that the Holy Spirit gave me a fresh revelation of my identity. I am a daughter of the King! If the president's daughter is favored, how much more are we favored!? Deuteronomy 28 is proof of this! Now wherever I go, I go knowing I am favored by GOD!

> *"I will make you into a great nation, and I will bless you; I will make your name great, and you will be a blessing.*
> —*Genesis 12:2*

Genesis 12 talks about the blessing of Abraham. That blessing is now upon us!

> *Christ hath redeemed us from the curse of the law, being made a curse for us: for it is written, Cursed is every one that hangeth on a tree: That the blessing of Abraham might come on the Gentiles through Jesus Christ; that we might receive the promise of the Spirit through faith.*
> —*Galatians 3:13-14*

Notes

Notes

Notes

HEALING

Healing is a topic that I am very passionate about. When I was nine-years-old, I was diagnosed with Alopecia Universalis. This is an autoimmune disease, which causes you to lose all of your hair. I knew, even then, that I served the Healer, but I was so unsure of how to attain that healing. I thought I had to attain healing by my works, by my own good behavior. It took me until I was about twenty-three years old to realize that Christ already paid the price for my healing.

Psalms 103:2-4 were some of the verses that spoke to me so very deeply. My heart grieves when I see the church sick. Sickness is something Christ paid for on the cross, and I pray that if you do not already believe that fact, you will believe it by the time you are finished reading this section. My hair has been restored to me. I am in awe of our God.

Bless the Lord, O my soul: and all that is within me, bless his holy name. Bless the Lord, O my soul, and forget not all his benefits: Who forgiveth all thine iniquities; who healeth all thy diseases;

who redeemeth thy life from destruction;
who crowneth thee with lovingkindness
and tender mercies.

—Psalms 103:1-4

My son, attend to my words; incline thine
ear unto my sayings. Let them not depart
from thine eyes; keep them in the midst of
thine heart. For they are life unto those that
find them, and health to all their flesh.

—Proverbs 4:20-22

The Word of God is alive and active. It is POWERFUL. Just by reading it, you can receive healing!

Do not be wise in your own eyes; fear the
LORD and shun evil. This will bring health
to your body and nourishment to your bones.

—Proverbs 3:7-8 (NIV)

When the Bible talks about the fear of the Lord, this does not mean fear in the sense of something being scary. This fear means to regard with reverence and awe. Fearing the Lord, or being in awe of Him, brings health to your body! Praise the Lord!

Then they cry unto the Lord in their trouble,
and he saveth them out of their distresses.
He sent his word, and healed them, and
delivered them from their destructions.
Oh that men would praise the Lord for his
goodness, and for his wonderful works to the

children of men!

—Psalms 107:19-21

And ye shall serve the Lord your God, and he shall bless thy bread, and thy water: and I will take sickness away from the midst of thee.

—Exodus 23:25

The Lord's will and desire is for His people to be well! He already paid the price for our healing!

O Lord my God, I cried unto thee, and thou hast healed me.

—Psalms 30:2

Surely he hath borne our griefs, and carried our sorrows: yet we did esteem him stricken, smitten of God, and afflicted. But he was wounded for our transgressions, he was bruised for our iniquities: the chastisement of our peace was upon him; and with his stripes we are healed.

— Isaiah 53:4-5
(Compare with Matthew 8:17. Jesus uses the words infirmities and sicknesses.)

Under the new covenant we are already healed; it is a finished work. We just need to believe and receive this free gift.

Who his own self bare our sins in his own body on the tree, that we, being dead to sins, should live unto righteousness: by whose

stripes ye were healed.
                                        —1 Peter 2:24

1 Peter 2:24 says we WERE healed. It is finished. Now, it is up to us to receive this free gift. Start thanking Him now for your healing.

That it might be fulfilled which was spoken by Esaias the prophet, saying, Himself took our infirmities, and bare our sicknesses.
                                        —Matthew 8:17

Matthew 8:17 is a reference to Isaiah 53:4. He bore our griefs and sorrows. The words *grief* and *sorrow* imply disease and pain!

The thief cometh not, but for to steal, and to kill, and to destroy: I am come that they might have life, and that they might have it more abundantly.
                                        —John 10:10

We need to start pointing the finger in the right direction. If something has been killed, stolen or destroyed, that is Satan—not Jesus. Jesus came to bring abundant life! He did not come to take our health; He came to heal us! He gave us authority and power. So when Satan comes in and tries to steal our health, we need to stand against it!

When the even was come, they brought unto him many that were possessed with devils: and he cast out the spirits with his word, and healed all that were sick.

—Matthew 8:16

Insomuch that they brought forth the sick into the streets, and laid them on beds and couches, that at the least the shadow of Peter passing by might overshadow some of them. There came also a multitude out of the cities round about unto Jerusalem, bringing sick folks, and them which were vexed with unclean spirits: and they were healed every one.

—Acts 5:15-16

And these signs shall follow them that believe; In my name shall they cast out devils; they shall speak with new tongues; They shall take up serpents; and if they drink any deadly thing, it shall not hurt them; they shall lay hands on the sick, and they shall recover.

—Mark 16:17-18

God commands believers to GO and heal the sick. His will is for His church to be living in health! We should be the ones who are healed—out healing those who do not know Him. He paid for our health on the cross!

Heal the sick, cleanse the lepers, raise the dead, cast out devils: freely ye have received, freely give.

—Matthew 10:8

Jesus Christ the same yesterday, and to day,

and for ever.

—*Hebrews 13:8*

Christ has not changed and will never change. His heart is for His people to be in health because He bore our sicknesses just as He bore our sins.

> *And, being assembled together with them, commanded them that they should not depart from Jerusalem, but wait for the promise of the Father, which, saith he, ye have heard of me. For John truly baptized with water; but ye shall be baptized with the Holy Ghost not many days hence.*
>
> —*Acts 1:4-5*

> *Believe me that I am in the Father, and the Father in me: or else believe me for the very works' sake. Verily, verily, I say unto you, He that believeth on me, the works that I do shall he do also; and greater works than these shall he do; because I go unto my Father.*
>
> —*John 14:11-12*

Have you ever wondered what the difference is between Christianity and every other religion? Power follows our words! We do not just speak about Christ, we have the power to do what He did (and even greater things). He sent the Holy Spirit to us; we now have that power living inside of us. He told His disciples to wait in Acts 1:4. He did not want them going out without the power! When we enter the room, Jesus enters the room. WOW! Mark 16:17 says that healing is a sign that should be following us. The power is in us!

> *And a woman having an issue of blood twelve years, which had spent all her living upon physicians, neither could be healed of any, Came behind him, and touched the border of his garment: and immediately her issue of blood stanched. And Jesus said, Who touched me? When all denied, Peter and they that were with him said, Master, the multitude throng thee and press thee, and sayest thou, Who touched me? And Jesus said, Somebody hath touched me: for I perceive that virtue is gone out of me. And when the woman saw that she was not hid, she came trembling, and falling down before him, she declared unto him before all the people for what cause she had touched him, and how she was healed immediately. And he said unto her, Daughter, be of good comfort: thy faith hath made thee whole; go in peace.*
> —Luke 8:43–48

For years, I compared myself to the sick woman in this story. I thought, *If I could only touch Him, I know I would be healed.* Then I began to realize that He is IN ME! I was comparing myself to the wrong person in the story. We are the ones with the power. He is in us and commanded us to heal the sick. People wanted to pass through Peter's shadow because they knew that just being near him was enough power for them to receive healing. The Lord gave us authority; He told us to go. People should be fighting to walk through OUR shadow, trying to touch the hem of OUR garments.

> *But that ye may know that the Son of man hath power on earth to forgive sins, (then saith he to the sick of palsy,) Arise, take up thy bed, and go unto thine house.*
> *—Matthew 9:6*

> *He healeth the broken in heart, and bindeth up their wounds.*
> *—Psalms 147:3*

> **Herein is our love made perfect, that we may have boldness in the day of judgment: because as he is, so are we in this world.**
> **—1 John 4:17**

As Christ is, so are we in this world. That is amazing! Christ is not in heaven sick, hurting or sad. That means we do not have to be either! He carried our griefs, sicknesses and sorrows upon the cross.

> *And Jesus went about all the cities and villages, teaching in their synagogues, and preaching the gospel of the kingdom, and healing every sickness and every disease among the people.*
> *—Matthew 9:35*

Is any sick among you? Let him call for the elders of the church; and let them pray over him, anointing him with oil in the name of the Lord: And the prayer of faith shall save the sick, and the Lord shall raise him up; and if he have committed sins, they shall be forgiven him.

—James 5:14-15

With long life will I satisfy him, and shew him my salvation.

—Psalms 91:16

Beloved, I wish above all things that thou mayest prosper and be in health, even as thy soul prospereth.

—3 John 2

For verily I say unto you, That whosoever shall say unto this mountain, Be thou removed, and be thou cast into the sea; and shall not doubt in his heart, but shall believe that those things which he saith shall come to pass; he shall have whatsoever he saith.

—Mark 11:23

Jesus did not tell us to speak to Him about our mountain. Instead, He told us to speak to our mountain about our God! Instead of begging God to heal you, thank him for already healing you, and then YOU command your sickness to go! Start talking to your mountain about your God!

And he cometh to Bethsaida; and they bring a blind man unto him, and besought him to touch him. And he took the blind man by the hand, and led him out of the town; and when he had spit on his eyes, and put his hands upon him, he asked him if he saw ought. And he looked up, and said, I see men as trees, walking. After that he put his hands again upon his eyes, and made him look up: and he restored, and saw every man clearly.
—Mark 8:22-25

The blind man was healed the first time Jesus touched him. It only takes one touch from Jesus to be changed. So why didn't the blind man see clearly the first time Jesus touched him? The man had to get rid of his unbelief. For years, he was blind. Could just one touch really give him sight? Do you believe? Or have doctors, experiences, and thoughts crept into your life and brought unbelief? Just like the blind man, maybe you need to leave the "town", and come to a place where it is just you and Jesus. Jesus IS our healer! It only takes one touch.

Now Peter and John went up together into the temple at the hour of prayer, being the ninth hour. And a certain man lame from his mother's womb was carried, whom they laid daily at the gate of the temple which is called Beautiful, to ask alms of them that entered into the temple; Who seeing Peter and John about to go into the temple asked an alms.

And Peter, fastening his eyes upon him with John, said, Look on us. And he gave heed unto them, expecting to receive something of them. Then Peter said, Silver and gold have I none; but such as I have give I thee: In the name of Jesus Christ of Nazareth rise up and walk. And he took him by the right hand, and lifted him up: and immediately his feet and ankle bones received strength.

—Acts 3:1-7

Delight thyself also in the Lord; and he shall give thee the desires of thine heart.

—Psalms 37:4

I shall not die, but live, and declare the works of the Lord.

—Psalms 118:17

No weapon that is formed against thee shall prosper; and every tongue that shall rise against thee in judgment thou shalt condemn. This is the heritage of the servants of the Lord, and their righteousness is of me, saith the Lord.

—Isaiah 54:17

Even after receiving full restoration to my body, I still claim these verses over my life. The thief will still come and try and take my health. Whenever I see hair falling out, I will start thanking God for healing me. I still listen to healing sermons almost every week and read over healing scriptures almost every day. The thief does not want you to maintain your confession, BUT he is defeated, and through Christ, YOU ARE VICTORIOUS! Healing is yours. Don't let the devil steal what Jesus purchased for you!

> *Fight the good fight of faith, lay hold on eternal life, whereunto thou art also called, and hast professed a good profession before many witnesses.*
> —*1 Timothy 6:12*

If you have read through this chapter and still have not seen your healing, it is not the Word of God that is at fault. The Word of God is clear; it is health to our entire bodies. His Word is true and constant. If you have not experienced healing, it is not God, it is you. It is the flesh getting in the way, whether it is unbelief or lack of knowledge. James 1:5 says, "If any of you lack wisdom, let him ask of God, that giveth to all men liberally, and upbraideth not; and it shall be given him." Ask the Lord why you have not been able to receive your healing, and He will show you. Healing is yours; it is paid for, and it is for today!

Notes

Notes

IDENTITY

Knowing our identity in Christ is crucial to having a victorious life. If Eve would have known her identity, she would not have been tempted by the devil. She was perfect, made in the image of the almighty God. If she knew that she was already perfect, blameless, and had everything she could ever need or want, she would have told the devil to leave. Instead, she questioned her identity.

As you read through this chapter, I pray that you will realize who you are in Christ. Next time the devil comes to tempt you with thoughts of inadequacy, tell him to leave! You are perfect—made in the image of an all-knowing, all-sufficient Creator who now dwells in you! Praise the Lord!

For by one sacrifice he has made perfect for ever them that are sanctified.
—Hebrews 10:14

But now the righteousness of God without the law is manifested, being witnessed by the law and the prophets; Even the righteousness of God which is by faith of Jesus Christ unto all and upon all them that believe: for there is no difference.

—Romans 3:21-22

For he hath made him to be sin for us, who knew no sin; that we might be made the righteousness of God in him.

—2 Corinthians 5:21

We are declared to be the righteousness of Christ. That is AMAZING! We can now go boldly before the throne. You should have no fear of death; He conquered death. When we meet Jesus, we meet Him blameless. Jesus took our judgment upon himself. Every single person's sins have already been forgiven and taken care of. The only sin that sends people to hell is: not believing on the name of Jesus Christ. Rest assured; you are righteous!

But ye are a chosen generation, a royal priesthood, an holy nation, a peculiar people; that ye should shew forth the praises of him who hath called you out of the darkness into his marvellous light.

—1 Peter 2:9

You are not only chosen, you are royal! You are in the family of God. There is no better family to be a part of.

Christ hath redeemed us from the curse of the law, being made a curse for us: for it is

written, Cursed is every one that hangeth on
a tree.
—Galatians 3:13

We are redeemed! We no longer have to live under the curse. Now, when Satan comes at you, know you have all the power and authority to trample him. No weapon formed against you will prosper.

And he that searcheth the hearts knoweth
what is the mind of the Spirit, because he
maketh intercession for the saints according
to the will of God.
—Romans 8:27

All throughout the New Testament, believers are referred to as saints. Despite their setbacks and failures, God still sees them as royal and set apart. Christ is interceding for His saints!

Nay, in all these things we are more than
conquerors through him that loved us.
—Romans 8:37

And we know that all things work together
for good to them that love God, to them who
are the called according to his purpose.
—Romans 8:28

Ye are the light of the world. A city that is set on an hill cannot be hid.
—Matthew 5:14

You are called according to God's purpose and are more than a conqueror. You have a light in you that cannot be hidden!

But as many as received him, to them gave he power to become the sons of God, even to them that believe on his name.
—John 1:12

Before I formed thee in the belly I knew thee; and before thou camest forth out of the womb I sanctified thee, and I ordained thee a prophet unto the nations.
—Jeremiah 1:5

Therefore if any man be in Christ, he is a new creature: old things are passed away; behold all things are become new.
—2 Corinthians 5:17

And the Lord shall make thee the head, and not the tail; and thou shalt be above only, and thou shalt not be beneath; if that thou hearken unto the commandments of the Lord thy God, which I command thee this day, to observe and to do them.
—Deuteronomy 28:13

You are healed, prosperous and powerful!

Christ has supplied everything you will ever need for an abundant life!

> *Behold, I give unto you power to tread on serpents and scorpions, and over all the power of the enemy: and nothing shall by any means hurt you.*
>
> *—Luke 10:19*

> *Nor height, nor depth, nor any other creature, shall be able to separate us from the love of God, which is in Christ Jesus our Lord.*
>
> *—Romans 8:39*

> *But God, who is rich in mercy, for his great love wherewith he loved us, Even when we were dead in sins, hath quickened us together with Christ, (by grace ye are saved).*
>
> *—Ephesians 2:4-5*

> ** Those who look to him are radiant; their faces are never covered with shame.*
>
> *—Psalms 34:5 (NIV)*

> *The Lord is on my side; I will not fear: what can man do unto me?*
>
> *—Psalms 118:6*

> *I can do all things through Christ which strengtheneth me.*
>
> *—Philippians 4:13*

> *You are of God, little children, and have overcome them: because greater is He that is*

in you, than He that is in the world.
—1 John 4:4

Herein is our love made perfect, that we may have boldness in the day of judgement: because as He is so are we in this world!
—1 John 4:17

But they that wait upon the Lord shall renew their strength; they shall mount up with wings as eagles; they shall run, and not be weary; and they shall walk, and not faint.
—Isaiah 40:31

You are strong and fearless. And with God on your side, you are unstoppable! Keep your eyes on Jesus. He is speaking to you and leading you. Trust Him, and He will work everything out for good.

Notes

Notes

JOY

Do people ever ask you, "Why are you so happy all the time?" People ask me that question often! Even when things are seemingly falling apart, all I can see is bright colors. It's almost as if I'm living in a bubble. But really, I'm living in the reality of Christ. He has filled us with so much joy. Look to Him; He has the answers. Even if you are in the midst of difficulty, know that He has already provided a way out! Start rejoicing— make the world wonder what is different about you!

> *Thou wilt shew me the path of life: in thy presence is fulness of joy; at thy right hand there are pleasures for evermore.*
> *—Psalms 16:11*

> *My lips shall greatly rejoice when I sing unto thee; and my soul, which thou hast redeemed.*
> *—Psalms 71:23*

> *When the Lord turned again the captivity of Zion, we were like them that dream. Then was our mouth filled with laughter, and our tongue with singing: then said they among*

*the heathen, The Lord hath done great things
for them. The Lord hath done great things for
us; whereof we are glad.*
— *Psalms 126:1-3*

*But the fruit of the Spirit is love, joy, peace,
longsuffering, gentleness, goodness, faith,
meekness, temperance: against such there is
no law.*
— *Galatians 5:22-23*

You have the Holy Ghost living in you—joy
is in you! Start praising the Lord, and draw that
out!

*Seven days shalt thou keep a solemn feast
unto the Lord thy God in the place which the
Lord shall choose: because the Lord thy God
shall bless thee in all thine increase, and in
all the works of thine hands, therefore thou
shalt surely rejoice.*
— *Deuteronomy 16:15*

*Then he said unto them, Go your way, eat the
fat, and drink the sweet, and send portions
unto them for whom nothing is prepared: for
this day is holy unto our Lord: neither be ye
sorry; for the joy of the Lord is your strength.*
— *Nehemiah 8:10*

*The hope of the righteous shall be gladness:
but the expectation of the wicked shall perish.*
— *Proverbs 10:28*

Now the God of hope fill you with all joy and peace in believing, that ye may abound in hope, through the power of the Holy Ghost.
—Romans 15:13

Whom having not seen, ye love; in whom, though now ye see him not, yet believing, ye rejoice with joy unspeakable and full of glory: Receiving the end of your faith, even the salvation of your souls.
—1 Peter 1:8-9

O clap your hands, all ye people; shout unto God with the voice of triumph.
—Psalms 47:1

You may be going through a difficult circumstance right now. It may be hard for you to 'feel' joy or to praise the Lord. Hebrews 13:15 tells us to offer a sacrifice of praise. Even when it is difficult, you can look to Jesus and begin to praise Him for all He has done for you. It is only a matter of time, and your situation will be turned around in your favor! Remember, we walk by faith and not by sight.

For his anger endureth but a moment; in his favour is life: weeping may endure for a night, but joy cometh in the morning.
—Psalms 30:5

There have been many times when I claimed Psalms 30:5 over my life. Things may be difficult for you right now, but joy comes in the morning! Start thanking Him for all He has done for you!

"The out-and-out Christian is a joyful Christian. The half-and-half Christian is the kind of Christian that a great many of you are—little acquainted with the Lord. Why should we live halfway up the hill and swathed in the mists, when we might have an unclouded sky and a radiant sun over our heads if we would climb higher and walk in the light of His face?"

—Alexander Maclare

Notes

Notes

PROSPERITY

I'm not here to preach the "prosperity gospel". I'm here to preach the only gospel. It just so happens that in the Word of God, it talks a lot about prosperity. The Lord's desire is for you to have an abundance! He does not want you in debt. He wants you so wealthy that you're not only paying your own bills, but you're paying your neighbor's too! Prosperity is not just for us; it's for the world. Money is not the root of all evil—the love of money is.

Honour the Lord with thy substance, and with the firstfruits of all thine increase: So shall thy barns be filled with plenty, and thy presses shall burst out with new wine.
*   —Proverbs 3:9–10*

For the Lord thy God blesseth thee, as he promised thee: and thou shalt lend unto many nations, but thou shalt not borrow; and thou shalt reign over many nations, but they shall not reign over thee. If there be among you a poor man of one of thy brethren within any of thy gates in thy land which the Lord thy God giveth thee, thou shalt not harden thine heart, nor shut thine hand from thy poor brethren: But thou shalt open thine hand wide unto him, and shalt surely lend him sufficient for his need, in that which he wanteth. Beware that there be not a thought in thy wicked heart, saying, The seventh year, the year of release, is at hand; and thine eye be evil against thy poor brother, and thou givest him nought and he cry unto the Lord against thee, and it be sin unto thee. Thou shalt surely give him, and thine heart shall not be grieved when thou givest unto him: because that for this thing the Lord thy God shall bless thee in all thy works, and in all that thou puttest thine hand unto.

—Deuteronomy 15:6-10

But this I say, He which soweth sparingly shall reap also sparingly; and he which soweth bountifully shall reap also bountifully. Every man according as he purposeth in his heart, so let him give; not grudgingly, or of necessity: for God loveth a cheerful giver. And God is able to make all grace abound toward you; that ye, always having all sufficiency in all things, may abound to every good work.

—2 Corinthians 9:6-8

Trusting God with your money should be one of the easiest things to do if you are saved. If you cannot trust the Lord with your finances, which are here one day and gone another, how can you trust Him with eternal life? If you can't offer your finances to the Lord, knowing He said He will supply all of your needs according to His riches, how can you offer Him your life and trust Him with eternity? If you are having trouble trusting Him with your finances, I would double check to see if you truly trust Him at all.

But my God shall supply all of your need according to his riches in glory by Christ Jesus.
—Philippians 4:19

Then Isaac sowed in that land, and received in the same year an hundredfold: and the Lord blessed him.
—Genesis 26:12

The Lord shall command the blessing upon thee in thy storehouses, and in all that thou settest thine hand unto; and he shall bless thee in the land which the Lord thy God giveth thee.
—Deuteronomy 28:8

The greedy stir up conflict, but those who trust in the Lord will prosper.
—Proverbs 28:25 (NIV)

Beloved, I wish above all things that thou mayest prosper and be in health, even as thy soul prospereth.
—3 John 2

And he shall be like a tree planted by the

rivers of water, that bringeth forth his fruit in his season; his leaf also shall not wither; and whatsoever he doeth shall prosper.

— *Psalms 1:3*

But thou shalt remember the Lord thy God: for it is he that giveth thee power to get wealth, that he may establish his covenant which he sware unto thy fathers, as it is this day.

—*Deuteronomy 8:18*

Let them shout for joy, and be glad, that favour my righteous cause: yea, let them say continually, Let the Lord be magnified, which hath pleasure in the prosperity of his servant.

—*Psalms 35:27*

The blessing of the Lord, it maketh rich, and he addeth no sorrow with it.

—*Proverbs 10:22*

It is a blessing to be able to be a blessing! It is a beautiful thing to have such an abundance to not only supply all of your own needs, but to be able to supply the needs of others. The Lord gives us the ability to prosper not merely for our own good, but for the good of sharing the Gospel.

For ye know the grace of our Lord Jesus Christ, that, though he was rich, yet for your sakes he became poor, that ye through his

poverty might be rich.
—2 Corinthians 8:9

Through the years, religion has taught many of us that it is the Lord that brings poverty and sickness upon us. We need to realize that it is the thief who comes to steal, kill, and destroy. Jesus came to bring an abundant life! Christianity is not a religion; it is a relationship with the Creator of the universe, the One who supplies our every need according to His riches in glory.

Riches and honour are with me; yea, durable riches and righteousness. My fruit is better than gold, yea, than fine gold; and my revenue than choice silver. I lead in the way of righteousness, in the midst of the paths of judgment: That I may cause those that love me to inherit substance; and I will fill their treasures.
—Proverbs 8:18-21

The thief cometh not, but for to steal, and to kill, and to destroy: I am come that they might have life, and that they might have it more abundantly.
—John 10:10

And Jesus answered and said, Verily I say unto you, There is no man that hath left house, or brethren, or sisters, or father, or mother, or wife, or children, or lands, for my sake, and the gospel's, But he shall receive an hundredfold now in this time, houses, and brethren, and sisters, and mothers, and children, and lands, with persecutions; and in the world to come eternal life.

—Mark 10:29-30

Bring ye all the tithes into the storehouse, that there may be meat in mine house, and prove me now herewith, saith the Lord of hosts, if I will not open you the windows of heaven, and pour you out a blessing, that there shall not be room enough to receive it.

—Malachi 3:10

Tithing is something that does not make sense to the world, but God promises His blessing upon those who give. Tithing is such a blessing. We cannot out-give God! We need to trust the Lord with every aspect of our lives, including our finances. He promises to supply all of our needs according to His riches.

According as his divine power hath given unto us all things that pertain unto life and godliness, through the knowledge of him that hath called us to glory and virtue: Whereby are given unto us exceeding great and precious promises: that by these ye might be partakers of the divine nature, having escaped the corruption that is in the world through lust.

—2 Peter 1:3-4

And the Lord was with Joseph, and he was a prosperous man; and he was in the house of his master the Egyptian. And his master saw that the Lord was with him, and that the Lord made all he did to prosper in his hand.
—Genesis 39:2-3

The Lord is no respecter of persons. If He prospers one person, He will do it for every person! He is the same yesterday, today, and forever. If it was good for Joseph to prosper, it is good for us to prosper. As prosperous people, we can give to the poor, feed the hungry, build homes, and travel with the good news of Jesus Christ.

This book of the law shall not depart out of thy mouth; but thou shalt meditate therein day and night, that thou mayest observe to do according to all that is written therein: for then thou shalt make thy way prosperous, and then thou shalt have good success.
—Joshua 1:8

And God is able to make all grace abound toward you; that ye, always having all sufficiency in all things, may abound to every good work.
—2 Corinthians 9:8

Jesus had so much money that He needed a treasurer (John 13:29). It is the love of money that is the root of all evil, not money itself (1 Timothy 6:10). Wouldn't it be awesome to have enough money to be able to abound to every good work just like 2 Corinthians 9:8 says? Being prosperous is not only for our benefit, but the benefit of others. When the Lord tells you to go on that mission trip, you can say, "No problem, Lord. I'm ready!" Whatever good work the Lord has for you, money won't even be an issue! God prospers us so that we can bless others.

Notes

Notes

PROTECTION

It is so beautiful to know that you are in the perfect plan of God. In His plan, you will be divinely protected.

Just like you believed and received salvation, you need to believe to receive protection. If you do not know the truth of divine protection, then it will not work for you. The truth will set you free! This requires knowing the truth. As you read through these scriptures, know that protection is your right as a child of God. You are protected, not just in your home, but everywhere you go. Claim His protection over your life today!

> *When thou passest through the waters, I will be with thee; and through the rivers, they shall not overflow thee: when thou walkest through the fire, thou shalt not be burned; neither shall the flame kindle upon thee.*
> *—Isaiah 43:2*

What a promise! The fire cannot burn us. The waters cannot overtake us! We are protected by the God of the universe. When Daniel was thrown into the lion's den, he was brought out without harm. When the three Hebrew children were cast into the fiery furnace, a fourth man appeared. God was with Daniel. He was with the three Hebrew children—and God is with us.

> *Then the king commanded, and they brought Daniel, and cast him into the den of lions. Now the king spake and said unto Daniel, Thy God whom thou servest continually, he will deliver thee.... My God hath sent his angel, and hath shut the lions' mouths, that they have not hurt me: forasmuch as before him innocency was found in me; and also before thee, O king, have I done no hurt.*
> —Daniel 6:16, 22

> *He answered and said, Lo, I see four men loose, walking in the midst of the fire, and they have no hurt; and the form of the fourth man is like the Son of God.*
> —Daniel 3:25

> *Have not I commanded thee? Be strong and of good courage; be not afraid, neither be thou dismayed: for the Lord thy God is with thee whithersoever thou goest.*
> —Joshua 1:9

Wherever you go, the King of Kings is with you. There is never any reason to fear! There is nothing that the world can do to us that Christ has not already overcome. He even tasted death for us so that we do not have to (Hebrews

2:9)! His amazing grace goes before us. We are protected. Be of good courage—Jesus is with you!

We are troubled on every side, yet not distressed; we are perplexed, but not in despair; Persecuted, but not forsaken; cast down, but not destroyed.
—2 Corinthians 4:8-9

The God of my rock; in him will I trust: he is my shield, and the horn of my salvation, my high tower, and my refuge, my saviour; thou savest me from violence. I will call on the Lord, who is worthy to be praised: so shall I be saved from mine enemies.
—2 Samuel 22:3-4

*He that dwelleth in the secret place of the most High shall abide under the shadow of the Almighty. I will say of the Lord, He is my refuge and my fortress: my God; in him will I trust. Surely he shall deliver thee from the snare of the fowler, and from the noisome pestilence. He shall cover thee with his feathers, and under his wings shalt thou trust: his truth shall be thy shield and buckler. Thou shalt not be afraid for the terror by night; nor for the arrow that flieth by day; Nor for the pestilence that walketh in darkness; nor for the destruction that wasteth at noonday. A thousand shall fall at thy side, and ten thousand at thy right hand; but it shall not come nigh thee. Only with thine eyes shalt thou behold and see the reward of

the wicked. Because thou hast made the Lord, which is my refuge, even the most High, thy habitation; There shall no evil befall thee, neither shall any plague come nigh thy dwelling. For he shall give his angels charge over thee, to keep thee in all thy ways. They shall bear thee up in their hands, lest thou dash thy foot against a stone. Thou shalt tread upon the lion and adder: the young lion and the dragon shalt thou trample under feet. Because he hath set his love upon me, therefore will I deliver him: I will set him on high, because he hath known my name. He shall call upon me, and I will answer him: I will be with him in trouble; I will deliver him, and honour him. With long life will I satisfy him, and shew him my salvation.
—Psalms 91

Psalms 91 is an amazing chapter. It is a great one to commit to memory. When the world is afraid that destruction is going to come on, you can stand on these verses. His angels have charge over you! No harm will come on your household. You are a child of God; you are protected. We need to know these truths in order to have them. Divine protection takes faith, and you can't have faith in what the Word says if you don't know what the Word says. You have to know the truth for it to make you free (John 8:32).

But let all those that put their trust in thee rejoice: let them ever shout for joy, because

*thou defendest them: let them also that love
thy name be joyful in thee.*
                                    —Psalms 5:11

*Thou art my hiding place; thou shalt preserve
me from trouble; thou shalt compass me about
with songs of deliverance. Selah.*
                                    —Psalms 32:7

*He holds success in store for the upright, he is
a shield to those whose walk is blameless, for
he guards the course of the just and protects
the way of his faithful ones. Then you will
understand what is right and just and
fair—every good path.*
                              —Proverbs 2:7-9 (NIV)

*My son, let not them depart from thine eyes:
keep sound wisdom and discretion: So shall
they be life unto thy soul, and grace to thy
neck. Then shalt thou walk thy way safely,
and thy foot shall not stumble.*
                              —Proverbs 3:21-23

Have you heard religious people talk about
being broken? Well, that is exactly what that is—
religion. That is contrary to what the scripture
teaches. The Lord keeps us from stumbling. He
is our protector. He binds our wounds (Psalms
147:3). He did not come to break us; He came
to heal us, protect us, comfort us, prosper us,
and whatever else it is that you need. He already
provided it!

The name of the Lord is a strong tower: the righteous runneth into it, and is safe.
—Proverbs 18:10

But the Lord is faithful, who shall stablish you, and keep you from evil.
—2 Thessalonians 3:3

Notes

Notes

POWER

In Luke 24:49, it says, "And now I will send the Holy Spirit, just as my Father promised. But stay here in the city until the Holy Spirit comes and fills you with power from heaven." This is where the power comes from. Even Christ had this power before He began His ministry. The Holy Spirit is a crucial element. If you are not filled with the Holy Spirit, then I would urge you not to wait—don't even leave where you are right now. Receive the Holy Spirit, AND THEN go. GO with the POWER—the power to heal the sick, the power to raise the dead, the power to lead the lost to our Savior. We need to be different from every other religious person. Power should be following us.

> *Confess your faults one to another, and pray one for another, that ye may be healed. The effectual fervent prayer of a righteous man availeth much.*
> —*James 5:16*

We are righteous through Christ (2 Corinthians 5:21), and because of that, our prayers are effective. When we pray, the Lord hears us. And in 2 Corinthians 1:20, it says that His answer is YES!

I am very passionate when it comes to politics. I feel that, as Christians, we need to be praying for wisdom and voting into office those whom Christ has called. Many times, I go to pray about our nation but then think, "There's no way my prayer can affect this." I was recently thinking about this, and the Holy Spirit placed James 5:15 on my heart. As a righteous people, our prayers ARE powerful, and Christ's answer is YES. We need to be in prayer about the big things—like abortion, the president, and this nation, as well as the things we deal with on a more personal level day to day. Christ's power is at work within us. We are an effective, powerful people through Christ. As Christians, we have a responsibility to speak up for those who do not have a voice. Do not be deceived. By not voting and not being involved in politics, you are taking a side.

> *For God hath not given us the spirit of fear; but of power, and of love, and of a sound mind.*
>
> —*2 Timothy 1:7*

If you are fearful, know that is not from God. He did not give us a spirit of fear. In the name of Jesus, command that fear to go!

> *But ye shall receive power, after that the*

Holy Ghost is come upon you: and ye shall be witnesses unto me both in Jerusalem, and in all Judaea, and in Samaria, and unto the uttermost part of the earth.
—Acts 1:8

I am so thankful the Holy Spirit is living in me. His power is strong in me. On our own, we are nothing, but thankfully, we are not on our own! We have the Holy One dwelling in us.

I can do all things through Christ which strengtheneth me.
—Philippians 4:13

Whatever Christ has called you to do, know that He has given you the power to be successful. Not to just make it through, but to prosper. Today, as you go about your day, know that Christ has given you the strength, not to just merely get through this day, but to excel!

*Now unto him that is able to do exceeding abundantly above all that we ask or think, according to the power that worketh in us.
—Ephesians 3:20

Behold, I give unto you power to tread on serpents and scorpions, and over all the power of the enemy: and nothing shall by any means hurt you.
—Luke 10:19

Can you imagine what life would be like if we believed this verse? Nothing by any means shall hurt you! Have you been 'hurt' recently by a co-worker, family member or friend? If we thought less about ourselves and more about others, people could not hurt us. Christ called us to die to self and live to righteousness. A dead person is not hurt by other people.

> *For our gospel came not unto you in word only, but also in power, and in the Holy Ghost, and in much assurance; as ye know what manner of men were among you for your sake.*
>
> —*1 Thessalonians 1:5*

> *But Jesus beheld them, and said unto them, With men this is impossible; but with God all things are possible.*
>
> —*Matthew 19:26*

Whatever you are believing for, know that nothing is impossible for the King of Kings.

> *And they were astonished at his doctrine: for his word was with power.*
>
> — *Luke 4:32*

We have that same power in our words. As He is, so are we in this world (1 John 4:17).

> *And being fully persuaded that, what he had promised, he was able also to perform.*
>
> —*Romans 4:21*

And my speech and my preaching was not with enticing words of man's wisdom, but in demonstration of the Spirit and of power.
—1 Corinthians 2:4

He giveth power to the faint; and to them that have no might he increaseth strength. Even the youths shall faint and be weary, and the young men shall utterly fall: But they that wait upon the Lord shall renew their strength; they shall mount up with wings as eagles; they shall run, and not be weary; and they shall walk, and not faint.
—Isaiah 40:29-31

I claim this verse over my life nearly every day. My youth is being renewed! His word WORKS!

According as his divine power hath given unto us all things that pertain unto life and godliness, through the knowledge of him that hath called us to glory and virtue.
—2 Peter 1:3

Notwithstanding the Lord stood with me, and strengthened me; that by me the preaching might be fully known, and that all the Gentiles might hear: and I was delivered out of the mouth of the lion.
—2 Timothy 4:17

Insomuch that they brought forth the sick into the streets, and laid them on beds and couches, that at the least the shadow of Peter

> *passing by might overshadow some of them.*
> —*Acts 5:15*

It only took Peter's shadow to cause their healing to manifest. God is the same yesterday, today, and forever. That same power is in us! Why then do many of us not see that at work in our lives? We are so saturated in the world. We need to give our lives to Christ, ridding ourselves of all unbelief. Many Christians want to spend five minutes in the Word every day and see huge results. Having people walk through your shadow and receive healing is going to take belief and ascending to the place where the Word takes precedence over your mind and body.

> *O God, thou art terrible out of thy holy places: the God of Israel is he that giveth strength and power unto his people. Blessed be God.*
> —*Psalms 68:35*

> **But if the Spirit of him that raised up Jesus from the dead dwell in you, he that raised up Christ from the dead shall also quicken your mortal bodies by his Spirit that dwelleth in you.**
> **—Romans 8:11**

> *And Stephen, full of faith and power, did great wonders and miracles among the people.*
> —*Acts 6:8*

Herein is our love made perfect, that we may have boldness in the day of judgment: because as he is, so are we in this world.
—1 John 4:17

For years, I was afraid of death because I knew I would be faced with judgment. I thought that Christ was going to shame me for all of the wrong I had done. This verse makes it so clear. His love is perfect toward us. We are already forgiven, and we can look forward to the day we meet our sweet Savior face to face! His perfect love casts out fear.

And what is the exceeding greatness of his power to us-ward who believe, according to the working of his mighty power, Which he wrought in Christ, when he raised him from the dead, and set him at his own right hand in the heavenly places.
—Ephesians 1:19-20

Having a form of godliness, but denying the power thereof: from such turn away.
—2 Timothy 3:5

Christians should be different from every other person. We have power that follows our words and actions!

And these signs shall follow them that believe; In my name shall they cast out devils; they shall speak with new tongues; They shall take up serpents; and if they drink any deadly

thing, it shall not hurt them; they shall lay
hands on the sick, and they shall recover.
                                    —*Mark 16:17–18*

This is not merely a suggestion—this is a command. Christianity should not be boring. It should be awesome! Have you laid your hands on any sick person lately?

Notes

Notes

SLEEP

Have you ever lain awake at night, wishing you could sleep. Well, I have good news for you—the Lord gives His beloved rest. And you, my friend, are His beloved.

> *I will both lay me down in peace, and sleep: for thou, Lord, only makest me dwell in safety.*
>
> *—Psalms 4:8*

> *It is vain for you to rise up early, to sit up late, to eat the bread of sorrows: for so he giveth his beloved sleep.*
>
> *—Psalms 127:2*

When thou liest down, thou shalt not be afraid: yea, thou shalt lie down, and thy sleep shall be sweet.
—Proverbs 3:24

He does not promise sweet sleep only when you have a comfortable bed. He promises that His beloved will have sweet rest. Circumstances must always bow to Jesus. Everything must bow to Jesus, therefore, it does not matter where you are or what the situation is. Believe that what these verses say are true, and take your restful night's sleep.

Notes

Notes

SPEECH

Our words are SO powerful. They have the power of life and death! When I was still sick, my words played such a vital part in me receiving my health. Mark 11:23 tells us to command our mountain to be thrown into the sea. We have to SPEAK it. I began to command my hair to grow; I commanded my mountain to move! I commanded sickness to go, and it went! Many of us are praying to God about our mountain rather than SPEAKING to our mountain about our God. Open your mouth and speak! Command your mountain to move, and it WILL move.

> *"Truly I tell you, if anyone says to this mountain, 'Go, throw yourself into the sea,' and does not doubt in their heart but believes that what they say will happen, it will be done for them."*
> *—Mark 11:23 (NIV)*

> *Let no corrupt communication proceed out of your mouth, but that which is good to the use of edifying, that it may minister grace unto the hearers.*
> *—Ephesians 4:29*

In the multitude of words there wanteth not sin: but he that refraineth his lips is wise. The tongue of the just is as choice silver: the heart of the wicked is little worth. The lips of the righteous feed many: but fools die for want of wisdom.

—*Proverbs 10:19-21*

Let the redeemed of the Lord say so, whom he hath redeemed from the hand of the enemy.
—*Psalms 107:2*

Let the redeemed of the Lord SAY so. We must say it. Psalms 22:3 says that He inhabits the praises of His people. As we praise Jesus, the atmosphere changes. Our situations may not change immediately, but our view of our situations will change. Christ has redeemed us from the curse. So when Satan begins to attack us, tell him we are redeemed. Get behind me Satan (Matthew 16:23)!

So then faith cometh by hearing, and hearing by the word of God.
—*Romans 10:17*

This verse defeats the argument that you do not need to say anything in order to share the gospel. While actions are very important, words are also necessary. Faith comes by hearing. We need to speak the truth. We also need to be sensitive about what we allow ourselves to listen to. Are you listening to songs with lyrics that speak death or life? Are you listening to TV shows or movies that are speaking truth? What you hear influences you. Make sure you are hearing and speaking truth.

Death and life are in the power of the tongue: and they that love it shall eat the fruit thereof.
—Proverbs 18:21

The power of life and death is yours. Are you speaking life to your situations, to your body, to those around you?

The wicked is snared by the transgression of his lips: but the just shall come out of trouble. A man shall be satisfied with good by the fruit of his mouth: and the recompence of a man's hands shall be rendered unto him.
—Proverbs 12:13-14

And they were astonished at his doctrine: for his word was with power.
—Luke 4:32

Therefore take no thought, saying, What shall we eat? or, What shall we drink? or, Wherewithal shall we be clothed?
—Matthew 6:31

You might be thinking about the worries of the world, like what you will wear or eat, but the Bible says do not SAY it. Know that the Creator of the world is taking care of you. When worries come your way, start speaking life, and watch your situation begin to change!

The mouth of a righteous man is a well of life: but violence covereth the mouth of the wicked.

—Proverbs 10:11

In the mouth of the foolish is a rod of pride: but the lips of the wise shall preserve them.
—Proverbs 14:3

He that keepeth his mouth keepeth his life: but he that openeth wide his lips shall have destruction.
—Proverbs 13:3

And Jesus said unto them, Because of your unbelief: for verily I say unto you, If ye have faith as a grain of mustard seed, ye shall say unto this mountain, Remove hence to yonder place; and it shall remove; and nothing shall be impossible unto you.
—Matthew 17:20

Jesus told us to speak to our mountain, and command it to move. Our words have the power to move mountains, to change situations, to bring life. He did not tell us to speak to Him about our mountain. Instead, He told us to speak to our mountain about Him. Let's begin to bring our praises to God instead of asking him to do things

He told us to do. It's a much more effective way to pray.

> *Beat your plowshares into swords and your pruning hooks into spears: let the weak say, I am strong.*
>
> *—Joel 3:10*

> *How long will ye vex my soul, and break me in pieces with words?*
>
> *—Job 19:2*

> *And seeing a fig tree afar off having leaves, he came, if haply he might find any thing thereon: and when he came to it, he found nothing but leaves; for the time of figs was not yet. And Jesus answered and said unto it, No man eat fruit of thee hereafter for ever. And his disciples heard it.*
>
> *—Mark 11:13-14*

When Jesus spoke to the fig tree, the disciples did not see any immediate results. They probably thought, *this guy is crazy! He's talking to trees!* In the physical, it did not look like anything changed. In reality, Jesus spoke to that fig tree, and it immediately yielded. It says in verse 20, "And in the morning, as they passed by, they saw the fig tree dried up from the roots." That fig tree died the moment Jesus spoke the words, but it took until the morning to see it.

Know that your words have power. When

you speak, the devil must yield. Keep thanking Him even if you do not see your fig tree wither immediately. Jesus is working from the roots, and you will see it. Thank Him while you wait. Use your words to thank Him for all He has done, for His great faithfulness to us. What He has promised will come to pass.

> *And God said, Let there be light: and there was light.*
> —*Genesis 1:3*

God did not just think the world into existence—He spoke it into existence. Don't just think about your problems; speak to them. Speak whatever it is that you need into existence. Life and death is in the power of the tongue. Choose life.

> *There is that speaketh like the piercings of a sword: but the tongue of the wise is health.*
> —*Proverbs 12:18*

> *A soft answer turneth away wrath: but grievous words stir up anger.*
> —*Proverbs 15:1*

> *Pleasant words are as an honeycomb, sweet to the soul, and health to the bones.*
> —*Proverbs 16:24*

> *That if thou shalt confess with thy mouth the Lord Jesus, and shalt believe in thine heart*

that God hath raised him from the dead, thou shalt be saved.
—*Romans 10:9*

He said to confess with your mouth that you believe in Jesus. When you speak the name of Jesus, situations change, strongholds break, and lives change!

Let the words of my mouth, and the meditation of my heart, be acceptable in thy sight, O Lord, my strength, and my redeemer.
—*Psalms 19:14*

That the communication of thy faith would become effectual by the acknowledging of every good thing which is in you in Christ Jesus.
—*Philemon 6*

Notes

Notes

Notes

RECEIVING CHRIST

How to become a child of God:

But as many as received him, to them gave he power to become the sons of God, even to them that believe on his name: Which were born, not of blood, nor of the will of the flesh, nor of the will of man, but of God.
—John 1:12-13

Jesus answered and said unto him, Verily, verily, I say unto thee, Except a man be born again, he cannot see the kingdom of God.
—John 3:3

For God so loved the world, that he gave his only begotten Son, that whosoever believeth in him should not perish, but have everlasting life. For God sent not his Son into the world to condemn the world; but that the world through him might be saved.
—John 3:16-17

According as he hath chosen us in him before the foundation of the world, that we should be holy and without blame before him in love: Having predestined us unto the adoption of

children by Jesus Christ to himself, according to the good pleasure of his will.
—Ephesians 1:4-5

That if thou shalt confess with thy mouth the Lord Jesus, and shalt believe in thine heart that God hath raised him from the dead, thou shalt be saved. For with the heart man believeth unto righteousness; and with the mouth confession is made unto salvation.
—Romans 10:9-10

Salvation is not complicated. You open your mouth, and you speak! Confess that the Lord died and rose again to save you. Believe it in your heart. That's it—it's that simple.

THINGS TO KNOW:

God loves you very much. He thought of you before the world was made. It is His intent that you be complete in Him, not lacking anything in life.

You can never do anything to make God love you more. You can never do anything to make God love you less.

God's not mad at you. He will never judge you for sins. He judged Jesus.

He gives power for you to be His child by believing in and receiving Jesus as Lord and

Savior of your life—through faith.

Now, if you are ready to receive Christ repeat this prayer:

Jesus, thank you that all my sins are forgiven, never to be remembered again. I receive You into my heart as Lord and Savior. I now make it my choice to live life as You direct through your Word and by Your Spirit. Thank you for salvation and all that it provides for me. Amen.

It's that simple! Welcome to the family!

Today's date: _____

Notes

Notes